4

Miyoshi
ピアノ・メソード

ピアノのための12の課題
三善晃　作曲

12 Progressive Propositions Piano Method
composed by Akira Miyoshi

edition **KAWAI**

皆様へのお願い
楽譜や歌詞・音楽書などの出版物を
権利者に無断で複製(コピー)することは、
著作権の侵害
(私的利用など特別の場合を除く)にあたり、
著作権法により罰せられます。
また、出版物からの不法なコピーが行われますと、
出版社は正常な出版活動が困難となり、
ついには皆様方が必要とされるものも
出版できなくなります。
音楽出版社と日本音楽著作権協会(JASRAC)は、
著作者の権利を守り、
なおいっそう優れた作品の出版普及に
全力をあげて努力してまいります。
どうか、不法コピーの防止に、
皆様方のご協力をお願い申し上げます。

カワイ出版
一般社団法人　日本音楽著作権協会

このメソードについて
About this method

ひとつの音をピアノでひくとき、
そこに音楽がうまれます。
ですから、すばらしいピアニストも、
ひとつの音をひくのにこころをこめます。
ピアノにはじめてふれるこどもたちにも、
たったひとつの音からでも
音楽がうまれることをあじわい、
じぶんのゆびが
その音をつむぎだすよろこびを、
しってもらいたいとおもいます。

このメソードは、
ピアノのれんしゅうが、どんなときでも、
音楽をうみ、音楽にふれ、
音楽をあじわうことであることを、
なによりもねがっています。
そのために、
ひとりひとりのこどものこころとからだが、
いつでもじぶんらしく、いきいきとして、
ピアノとなかよくなれるように、
そして、せんせいとこどもたちがいっしょに
たのしみながらレッスンできるように、
かんがえ、さっきょくし、くみたてました。

プロポジションとは、
「ていあん(提案)」とか
「めいだい(命題)」といういみですが、
ここでは、こどもたちがピアノをひきながら
すすんでいく「12のせかい(世界)」と、
かんがえてください。

When you play a note on the piano, your musical journey begins. This is also the beginning of the joy of creating your very own musical world.

I developed this method with the hope that every time you play the piano, you will feel, taste and fully enjoy music.

These 12 propositions will take you to 12 wonderful worlds of piano playing.

先生がたへ
このメソードの12のプロポジションが
「提案」している「命題」は、

1. すべての楽譜が生きた音楽であること。
2. ピアノの表現力を
   いままでの慣習や常識に閉じ込めないこと。
3. 子供の可能性に積極的に触れること。
4. のびのびとした雰囲気のなかで
   将来のためになる心身の体験を
   取り込むことです。

その意味で、
左手は伴奏という考え方でなく、
左手にもポリフォニーの表情を与え、
難しいとされる技術も大胆に、
同時に合理的に取り入れています。

最後に、
いわゆる難易度の段階は絶対的なものでなく、
一人一人の子供の
心身の個性、興味、志向性に応じて、
先生がたが
プロポーズ(提案)してくださいますよう、
お願いします。

To the teacher
This method aims to improve the following aspects through 12 propositions :

1. All the pieces provide vivid musicality.
2. Allow freedom of expression.
3. Believe in the possibility (potential) of your pupil.
4. Provide a meaningful experience leading to future   development.

and adopt various musical techniques confidently and practically, such as polyphonic lines on the left hand part.

Please guide your pupils through the stages freely, and propose the pieces according to their abilities.

volume4のカリキュラムについて
About Volume 4 Curriculum

この第4プロポジションから、
プロポジションごとに♯と♭を一つずつおぼえていきます。

第4プロポジションでは、ファ♯で、**ト長調とホ短調**を練習します。
また、**指かえし**の第一段階に入ります。

【導入編】
もう一度、鍵盤図と楽譜を対照させ、黒鍵ファ♯を紹介します。
1→3、3→1の指かえしの初めての体験にも入ります。

【基本編】
冒頭で、**1→3、3→1の基礎ドリル**を各種リズム・パターンで行ない、**練習曲47**までにその起動力を高めます。
練習曲48からは、それに**1→4、4→1**を加え、同じようにパターン練習をします。
練習曲52からは、その指かえし技術を使ってト長調の音楽を導入します。

【発展編】
ハ長調とト長調の音楽で、曲の規模を少しずつ拡大し、主題と楽想への関心を高めていきます。
音楽の構造性についても、気づいてもらいましょう。

【応用編】
練習曲63までは、イ短調とホ短調を加え、
左手右手それぞれの重音のリズム奏を交えた合奏曲で、
音楽体験の幅を広げるとともに、多様な楽想に触れ、表現の
自発的な工夫を促します。
練習曲64、練習曲65、練習曲66は、それぞれのレガート奏法を
工夫しながら、**2声ポリフォニー**の楽曲を弾きますが、
これらは小さなピアニストのレパートリーになるでしょう。

【楽典】
「おんぷのなかまたち」とこの「楽典」は、今までに弾いた曲を実例にして、常に音楽を耳で聴き、実感させながら
理解させてあげてください。

Volume 4 curriculum
In this proposition, new keys are introduced.

In Proposition 4, F♯ is introduced with G major and E minor.
Also, pupils learn the first step of crossing fingers

Introduction
F♯ is introduced once again, linked to the keyboard chart and music.
Experience of Crossing fingers 1 → 3 and 3 → 1 begins.

Basic exercises
Practicing 1 → 3 and 3 → 1 technique with various rhythm patterns, which leads to 1 → 4 and 4 → 1 technique with the same practice from Preliminary Exercise 48.
A new key, G major, is introduced in Preliminary Exercise 52 using the technique of crossing fingers.

Developing Skills
Playing larger pieces in C major and G major, keeping in mind the theme and the character of the piece, while drawing attention to the structure of music.

Applications
Playing various types of ensemble pieces that include double-notes with each of the left and right hands, in A minor and E minor. This is to expand pupils' musical experience and help them to conceive their original expression.
With Preliminary Exercises 64, 65 and 66, they play two-voice polyphonic pieces, that will be a good repertoire pieces for young pianists.

Theory
Use "Friends of notes" and the Theory here to have pupils always listen to the actual music to understand. -

Proposition 4

ゆびのかえしと ファ♯

1のゆびが、 3のゆびや、 4のゆびの、

むこうどなりにいったり、

3のゆびや、 4のゆびが、 1のゆびの、

こちらどなりにきたりして、

たくさんのけんばんを、

つづけてひくことができます。

Crossing the fingers and F♯
Crossing the fingers is to move the finger 1 going under finger 3 or 4, or fingers 3 and 4 going over finger 1. Using these fingerings, you can play many keys continuously.

もくじ
Contents

曲名
title

ピアノをひくまえの準備運動
Warm-up exercises before playing

- **1** いすにすわるまえに、身体と呼吸の練習をしましょう ……… 8
  1. Body and breathing exercises before sitting down
- **2** いすにすわって、すわる姿勢の練習をしましょう ……… 8
  2. How to sit with the right posture
- **3** 鍵盤にさわってみましょう ……… 9
  3. Let's touch the keyboard

導入編
Introduction

- けんばんと おんぷの かんけい ……… 10
  Relationship between keys and notes
- こっけん ……… 11
  Black notes
- ひいてみましょう ……… 11
  Let's try to play
- ファ♯ ……… 12
  F♯
- ひいてみましょう ……… 12
  Let's try to play
  - ■ ファ♯ こんにちは　Hello, F♯ ……… 13
  - ■ ファ♯のまわり　ト長調のコラール　Around F♯ Choral in G major ……… 14
  - ■ ファ♯のまわり　ホ短調のコラール　Around F♯ Choral in E minor ……… 14
  - ■ ファ♯のまわり　ニ長調のワルツ　Around F♯ Waltz in D major ……… 15
  - ■ ファ♯からの昇り降り　Up and down from F♯ ……… 16
- おんぷきごう ……… 17
  Clefs
- ひいてみましょう ……… 17
  Let's try to play
- **練習曲 41a** みぎての ゆびかえし 3-① 1-③　みぎてでおとなり3 ……… 18
  41a Crossing right-hand fingers 3-① 1-③　Fingers 1 and 3 next to each other
- **練習曲 41b** ひだりての ゆびかえし 3-① 1-③　ひだりてでおとなり3 ……… 19
  41b Crossing left-hand fingers 3-① 1-③　Fingers 1 and 3 next to each other
- **練習曲 41c** りょうての ゆびかえし 3-① 1-③　りょうてでおとなり3 ……… 20
  41c Crossing both-hand fingers 3-① 1-③　Fingers 1 and 3 next to each other on both hands

基本編
Basic exercises

- **練習曲 42** みぎての ゆびかえし 3-① 1-③の変奏　虹は7色（右手） ……… 22
  42 Variations on crossing fingers 3-① 1-③ of the right hand　Seven colors of the rainbow (right hand)
- **練習曲 43** ひだりての ゆびかえし 3-① 1-③の変奏　虹は7色（左手） ……… 24
  43 Variations on crossing fingers 3-① 1-③ of the left hand　Seven colors of the rainbow (left hand)
  - ■ ゆっくりミとファ　Slowly, E and F ……… 26
  - ■ ゆっくりソとラ　Slowly, G and A ……… 27
- **練習曲 44a** みぎての ゆびかえし 3-① 1-③の復習　ミとファでかえし ……… 28
  44a Review of crossing fingers 3-① 1-③ of the right hand　Crossing the fingers on E and F
- **練習曲 44b** ひだりての ゆびかえし 3-① 1-③の復習　ラとソでかえし ……… 28
  44b Review of crossing fingers 3-① 1-③ of the left hand　Crossing the fingers on A and G
- **練習曲 44c** りょうての ゆびかえし 3-① 1-③の復習　いっしょにかえし ……… 29
  44c Review of crossing fingers 3-① 1-③ of both hands　Crossing the fingers of both hands
- **練習曲 45** ゆびかえしで やまと なみ を　おおきいやま よせるなみ ……… 30
  45 Making a mountain and a wave by crossing fingers　A big mountain and surging waves
  - ■ ミとファ、ソとラ、なめらかに（イ短調）　E and F, G and A, smoothly (A minor) ……… 32
  - ■ ミとファ、ソとラ、なめらかに（ハ長調）　E and F, G and A, smoothly (C major) ……… 33
- **練習曲 46** ゆびかえしの やまのぼり　やっと ついた! ……… 34
  46 Climbing the mountain by crossing fingers　Finally we made it!
- **練習曲 47** ゆびかえしの サーフィン　すてきに のれた! ……… 36
  47 Let's surf by crossing fingers　Enjoy the wave with spirit!
- **練習曲 48** みぎての ゆびかえし
  48 Crossing fingers

    3-①　と　1-③　をつかって　そら たかく ……… 38
    　　　　　　　1-④　　　　　　 The sky is so high!
    3-①　1-③　of the right hand
    　　　1-④

曲名
title

練習曲49　ひだりての ゆびかえし
49 Crossing the fingers

　　　　　　3-① と ¹-③ をつかって
　　　　　　　　　　 ¹-④
　　　　3-① ¹-③ of the left hand
　　　　　　 ¹-④

うみ ふかく ──────── 39
The sea is so deep

練習曲 50　みぎての ゆびかえし 4-① 1-④の変奏
50 Variations on crossing fingers 4-① 1-④ of the right hand

かぜも 7色(右手) ──────── 40
The wind and seven colors (right hand)

練習曲51　ひだりての ゆびかえし 4-① 1-④の変奏
51 Variations on crossing the finger 4-① 1-④ of the left hand

かぜも 7色(左手) ──────── 42
The wind and seven colors (left hand)

練習曲 52a　みぎてで ファ♯（シャープ）
52a F♯ with the right hand

シャープさん こんにちは(右手) ── 44
Hello, ♯! (right hand)

練習曲 52b　ひだりてで ファ♯（シャープ）
52b F♯ with the left hand

シャープさん こんにちは(左手) ── 45
Hello, ♯! (left hand)

練習曲 52c　ファ♯（シャープ）と 1-③ 3-①のれんしゅう
52c F♯ and 1-③ 3-① practice

ちいさな うずまき ──────── 46
Little swirl

練習曲 52d　ファ♯（シャープ）と 4-① 1-④のうんどうのれんしゅう
52d F♯ and 1-④ 4-① practice

みんなで いこう! ──────── 47
Come on, everyone!

練習曲 52e　りょうてで ファ♯（シャープ）
52e F♯ on both hands

ゆうやけ おやすみ ──────── 48
Good night, sunset

発展編
Developing skills

練習曲 53　なめらかな ハ長調のうた
53 A gentle song in C major

なみの いきき ──────── 50
Waves are going and coming

練習曲 54　ト長調で 1-②-①のれんしゅう
54 Practicing 1-②-① in G major

やさしい つむじかぜ ──────── 51
Gentle whirlwind

練習曲 55　ながいレガート
55 Long legato

すいへいせん ──────── 52
Horizone

練習曲 56　ゆびを じゆうにうつす
56 Shifting fingers

かぜの ものがたり ──────── 53
The story of the wind

練習曲 57　主題の旋律
57 Melody of the theme

よろこびの うた ──────── 54
Joyful song

練習曲 58　なめらかな ト長調のうた
58 A flowing song in G major

帆と かぜの うた ──────── 56
The sail and the wind

応用編
Applications

練習曲 59　ハ長調で 左手の重音のリズム奏
59 Rhythmic double notes in C major, left hand

あさかぜ のうた ──────── 58
The morning wind

練習曲 60　イ短調で 右手の重音のリズム奏
60 Rhythmic double notes in A minor, right hand

ゆうひ のうた ──────── 59
The sunset

練習曲 61　左手で 重音を使って合奏
61 Ensemble using double notes, left hand

ワルツの輪 ──────── 60
Circle of the Waltz

練習曲 62　ト長調で 右手の重音の旋律奏
62 Melodic double notes in G major, right hand

リングの舞い ──────── 62
Dance of the ring

練習曲 63　ホ短調で 右手の重音の旋律奏
63 Melodic double notes in E minor, right hand

茜色のエレジー ──────── 64
Elegy on crimson

　　復習　　おんぷの なかまたち ──────── 66
　　Preview　　Friends of notes

　　　　　　8 ぶんおんぷと 8 ぶんきゅうふ ──────── 67
　　　　　　Eighth notes and rests

8 ぶんおんぷと 8 ぶんきゅうふの ながさのかんけい ──────── 67
Relationship between eighth notes and rests

練習曲 64　ト長調のうた
64 A song in G major

みぃつけた 川辺 のはな ──────── 68
Flowers along the riverside

練習曲 65　ホ短調のうた
65 A song in E minor

かなしみ おやすみ ──────── 69
Goodnight, sadness

練習曲 66　ト長調の対位法
66 Counterpoint in G major

いきかう よろこび ──────── 70
Joy comes and goes

練習曲 67　ホ短調で両手のうた
67 A song in E minor for both hands

かなしみのうみ、なぐさめの かぜ ── 72
Sea of sorrow, wind of comfort

楽典
Theory

おんがくの ことばとやくそく ──────── 74
Musical terms and rules

8 第4プロポジション
No. 4 Proposition

ピアノをひくまえの準備運動
Warmup exercises before playing

せんせいによんでいただいて、じゅんびうんどうをしましょう。
Exercise with your teacher

❶ いすにすわるまえに、身体と呼吸の練習をしましょう
Body and breathing exercise before sitting down

1. 両足を肩幅にひらき、まっすぐ立って、
   ゆっくり息をはきながら肩を上げる。
   腕は力を抜いて自然に下へさげたまま。
2. 息を全部はいたら肩を上げたまま息をとめて3つ数える。
3. 肩をストンと落とし、同時に息をスッと吸う。
   この時の肩と腕の感じを覚える。
   これを何回もくりかえす。

1. Stand upright with legs shoulder width apart.
   Start breathing out slowly and lift the shoulders up while both arms remain relaxed.
2. With your breath exhaled and your shoulders still raised, count to three slowly.
3. Drop the shoulders to the original position and inhale at the same time. Try to remember this feeling of release and repeat the action.

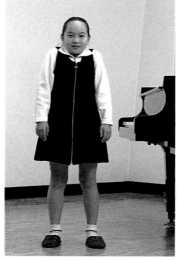

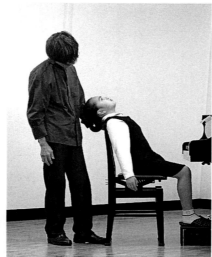

❷ いすにすわって、すわる姿勢の練習をしましょう
How to sit with the right posture

1. いすの前端と膝の内側に、にぎりこぶしが楽に入る程度に腰かける。
2. **いすの高さ**…いすにすわって、下腕を水平に曲げた肘の下の線が、
   白鍵の上面と同じ高さになるように。
3. **いすの位置**…手のひらを鍵盤の上にかざしたとき、
   肘が体側線から白鍵の前面までの間の約$\frac{1}{3}$になるように。
4. 踏台の高さは垂直におろした左足がピタリとつくように。
5. 上体は❶の3の感じで力を抜き、右足は踏みしめず楽な感じで。
6. 首を上下に動かす。鍵盤を見ながら左右に動かす。
7. 左足を軽く踏みしめて、上体を前後・左右にゆらす。力が入らないように。

1. Allow enough space for a clenched fist between the edge of the stool and the back of your knee.
2. **The height of the stool**
   Sit on the stool. Place the lower arms horizontally so the elbows are at the same level as the white keyboard.
3. **Position of the stool**
   Place your hands on the keyboard.
   Your elbows should be one-third of the distance from your center of the body to the edge of the white keys.
4. Your legs should be at a 90 degree angle, with the height of the footstool adjusted so the left foot is flat.
5. The upper part of the body and your right foot should be as relaxed as they were in ❶-3.
6. Move your neck up and down. Move your head right to left with your eyes on the keyboard.
7. Step the left foot little firmly, and sway the upper part of the body, both up and down and left to right. Do this exercise in a relaxed manner.

❸鍵盤にさわってみましょう
Let's touch the keyboard

1 ❶の**3**の状態から手のひらを下にして鍵盤の上にかざす。

2 肩、上腕、手首、指の力を抜き、手首から先を自然に下にたらす。
五本の指は、空気の球をそっと包む感じになる。
親指も力を入れず内側に向くように(外側にそらせないこと)。
この形をよくおぼえる。
1、**2**をくりかえす。

3 空気の球をつぶさないようにして、指を鍵盤の上におく。
手首は空気の球の高さより下げすぎない
(手首が凹まないように)。
指の関節は、みな凸型になっている。
この形をよくおぼえる。

1 With the upper part of your body as relaxed as it was in ❶-**3**, hold your hands over the keyboard.

2 Your shoulder, upper arm, wrist and fingers remain relaxed and your hands hang down naturally. It's like you are holding a ball of air in your hands.
Your thumb, without forcing it, is slightly bent towards your little finger.
Remember this shape and repeat the action.

3 Keep the round shape of your hands and slowly put them on the keyboard.
Look at and remember the position of your wrists and finger joints.

けんばんと おんぷの かんけい
Relationship between keys and notes

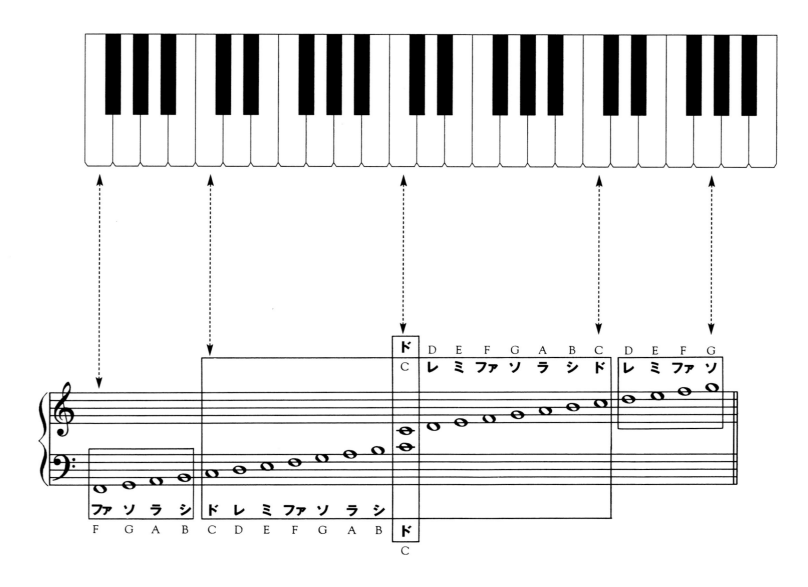

先生がたへ
白鍵で7この音名とオクターヴのイメージを実感させてください。
To the teacher
Help your pupil to grasp the image of an octave and note names.

こっけん
Black notes

> **はっけん** のことは、わかりましたね。
> こんどは、**こっけん** のことを、おぼえましょう。
> Now, let's learn about the black notes

はっけんの右どなりの**こっけん**は、その**はっけん** の ♯（シャープ）とよびます。

ファの右どなりの**こっけん** は、**ファ**♯（ファ・シャープ）とよびます。

ファ♯は、ファとソの **まんなかのたかさのおと**です。

A black note that is to the right of a white note is called the ♯ (sharp) of the white note.
Therefore, the black note that is to the right of F is called F ♯.
The pitch of F ♯ is between F and G.

   ほかの **ド**♯ （ド・シャープ） C♯

       レ♯ （レ・シャープ） D♯

       ソ♯ （ソ・シャープ） G♯

       ラ♯ （ラ・シャープ）もおなじです。 A ♯ are the same.

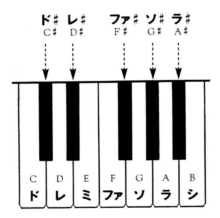

ひいてみましょう
Let's try to play!

ファ♯
F♯

ファの みぎどなりのこっけんが、ファ♯（ファ・シャープ）で、おとはファよりも たかくなります。
The black key that is to the right of F is called F♯ and its pitch is higher than F.

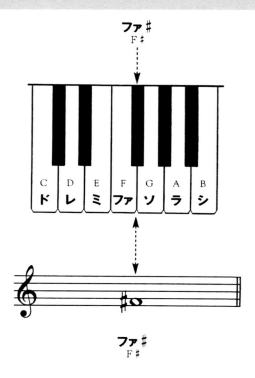

ひいてみましょう
Let's try to play

先生がたへ
ここでは♯の約束だけです。ファ、ファ♯、ソを弾いて（弾かせて）音の上向を感得させてください。
左手の2小節目のファには、♯がついていないことに気づかせてください。♮記号は、後でおぼえます。

To the teacher
Show your pupil that the pitch goes higher by playing F, F♯ and G.
Draw their attention that the F note played with the left hand in the second bar is not with ♯.
♮ will be explained later.

ファ♯ こんにちは
Hello, F♯

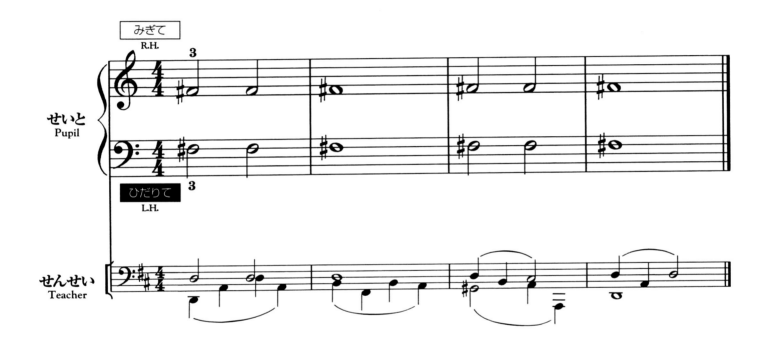

先生がたへ
片手ずつ、それから両手、という順序でも。2、4、1、5の指でも弾きましょう。
To the teacher
The pupil can practice hands separately first, and hands together. 2, 4, 1, 5 fingering is also advised.

ファ♯のまわり　ト長調のコラール
Around F♯ Choral in G major

ファ♯のまわり　ホ短調のコラール
Around F♯ Choral in E minor

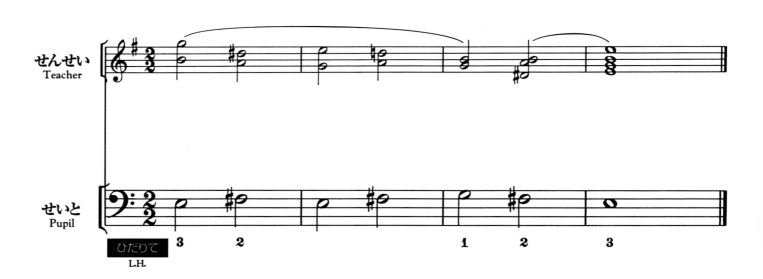

先生がたへ
どちらの曲も3の指から弾き始める指使いを4-3-4-3-2-3-4 や 5-4-5-4-3-4-5のように変えて弾かせてください。
For teachers
Other fingering, e.g. 4-3-4-3-2-3-4, or 5-4-5-4-3-4-5, is advised for practice.

ファ♯のまわり ニ長調のワルツ
Around F♯ Waitz in D major

先生がたへ
同じ旋律を片手ずつ練習します。同音連打でのこのリズムは、不安定になりがちです。
先生の合奏に乗ってスムーズなワルツ・テンポで。
To the teacher
Both hands play the same melody, but practice should start from hands separately.
Keep smooth movement of Waltz.

ファ♯からの昇り降り
Up and down from F♯

先生がたへ
レガート奏で、同じ呼吸で。
To the teacher
Always legato, with breathing.

おんぶきごう
Clefs

きょくのなかの **ぜんぶのファ**に ♯ (シャープ)をつけてひくおんがくでは、
五せんの はじめの**ファ**のところに ♯ (**44**ページ参照)をつけておきます。
When all Fs are played as F♯ in a piece, the ♯ is written at the beginning of the staves, next to the clef mark (refer to page 44).

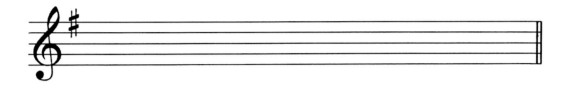

ひいてみましょう
Let's try to play

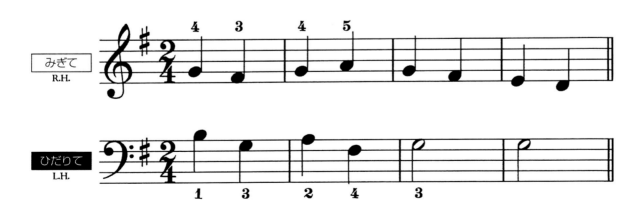

先生がたへ
この導入編では、ファ♯の黒鍵にふれて、なじませるだけで結構です。

To the teacher
In this introduction, just have your pupil get used to F♯ on the black key.

第4プロポジション
No. 4 Proposition

練習曲 41a みぎての ゆびかえし 3-① 1-③
みぎてで おとなり 3
41a Crossing right-hand fingers 3-① and 1-③
Fingers 1 and 3, next to each other

まず、**みぎて**の れんしゅうです。
おとを つづけてひきながら、
たかい ほうへ
ひくい ほうへ
てのばしょを うつしていくために、
ゆびのかえしを れんしゅうしましょう。

Let's start with the right hand.
Practice crossing the fingers in order to change the position of
the hand higher and lower.

せんせいによんでいただきましょう。
Your teacher will explain this to you.

3から① へは、1のゆびが3のゆびの下をくぐります。
1から③ へは、3のゆびが1のゆびの上をまたぎます。
①、③のおとだけが、つよくならないように。

From 3 to ①, finger 1 goes under finger 3.
From 1 to ③, finger 3 goes over finger 1.
Avoid playing ① and ③ too strongly.

先生がたへ
1) このメソードでは、指かえしの場所で、その指の数字を○で囲って表示します。
2) 親指が、外側にそらないように。
3) 指かえしのとき、手首をまわしすぎないように。
To the teacher
1) The number with the circle shows the finger that is crossing.
2) When crossing the finger, make sure the thumb is kept inward.
3) When crossing the fingers, avoid twisting the wrist too much.

第4プロポジション
No. 4 Proposition

練習曲 41b ひだりての ゆびかえし 3-① 1-③
ひだりてで おとなり 3

41b Crossing left-hand fingers 3-① and 1-③
     Fingers 1 and 3 next to each other

ひだりても、
ゆびのかえしをつかって
てのばしょをうつせるようにしましょう。

Now with the left hand,
change the hand's position by crossing the fingers.

せんせいによんでいただきましょう。
Your teacher will explain this to you.

こんどは、ひだりてです。
3から①へは、1のゆびが3のゆびの下をくぐります。
1から③へは、3のゆびが1のゆびの上をまたぎます。
①、③のおとだけが、つよくならないように。

Now try on the left-hand.
From 3 to ①, finger 1 goes under finger 3.
From 1 to ③, finger 3 goes over finger 1.
Avoid playing ① and ③ too strongly.

第4プロポジション
No. 4 Proposition

練習曲 41c　りょうてのゆびかえし3-①　1-③
りょうてで おとなり 3
41c Crossing both-hand fingers 3-① and 1-③
　　Fingers 1 and 3 next to each other of both hands

はじめに **みぎて** だけ、
つぎに **ひだりて** だけでひいて、
よくおぼえてから、あわせてひきましょう。

Firstly, play the right hand part,
then the left hand part.
When you are ready, play with both hands.

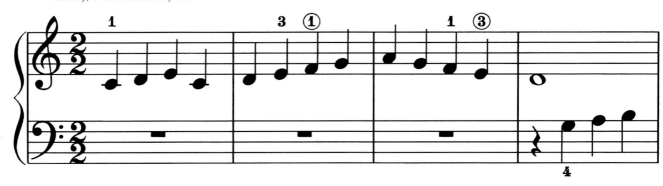

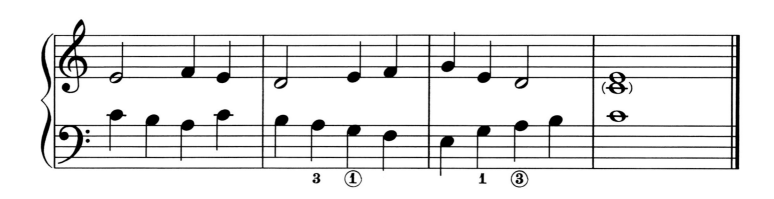

先生がたへ
この練習曲は、基本編の練習曲42・43・44をさらってから弾かせてもよいでしょう。
To the teacher
This piece may also be played after learning exercises 42, 43 and 44 in the Basic exercises

基本編
Basic exercises

いろいろな

ピアノのきょくをひくために、

ゆびのつかいかたを くふうします。

せんりつを、つづけてひくためには、

①のゆびを、ちゅうしんにした

ゆびかえしが、やくだちます。

For playing various pieces,
fingerings are important.
Crossing the fingers using finger 1
is very useful for playing a melody smoothly.

せんせいによんでいただきましょう。
Your teacher will explain this to you.

ゆびかえしをするとき
・おやゆびを、やわらかく、うちがわにまわします。
・てくびを、まげないように。
・**ゆびかえし**をするとき、1、3、4のゆびで、てのおもさを、
　おなじようにかんじること。
・おとをきいて、つよさが、かわらないようにちゅういします。
・おとをきいて、**せんりつ**が、とぎれないようにちゅういします。

When crossing your fingers,
・ The thumb should be relaxed. Relax and turn the thumb inward.
・ The wrist is not bent.
・ The hand's weight is supported equally by the fingers 1, 3 and 4.
・ Avoid unnecessary accents.
・ Play the melody smoothly connected.

第4プロポジション
No. 4 Proposition

練習曲 42　みぎての　ゆびかえし 3-① 1-③の変奏

虹は7色（右手）

42 Variations on crossing fingerss 3-① 1-③ of the right hand
Seven colors of the rainbow (right hand)

おなじせんりつを、いろいろなひょうしとリズムでひきましょう。
ゆびかえしのばしょは　おなじですが、
すばやくしなければならない**きょく**もあります。
せいかくなリズムで　ひいてください。

Let's play the same melody in different rhythms and times.
In some pieces, you need to cross the fingers quickly.
Keep the accurate rhythm.

先生がたへ
練習曲42も、全部つづけて弾かせなくてもよいでしょう。しかし、リズムの変容に興味を示す生徒もいます。
その場合は、挑戦させてください。ほかのリズムを工夫する生徒もいるかもしれません。
8分の6拍子が出てきますが、先生が弾きながら拍子（1小節2拍）どりしてあげるなど、運動イメージを実感させてください。

To the teacher
In this exercise, there is no need to play all the pieces continuously. But if a pupil is interested in different rhythms, you can let them try.
Some pupils may even play with new rhythms. When playing the 6/8 pieces, you can help them feel the rhythm by tapping the beat.

第4プロポジション
No. 4 Proposition

練習曲 43 ひだりての ゆびかえし 3-① 1-③の変奏
虹は7色（左手）
43 Variations on crossing fingers 3-① 1-③ of the left hand
Seven colors of the rainbow (left hand)

こんどは、ひだりてです。
はじめに 1 を よくおぼえてから、2 から 7 に すすみましょう。

Now, let's try with the left hand.
Start with piece 1, and when you are ready, move on to 2 to 7.

ゆっくり ミとファ
Slowly, E and F

先生がたへ
3-①, 1-③は、ゆっくり指かえしをしますが、かえした音がゴツゴツしないよう、全体をレガートでなだらかに。
To the teacher
Always keep smooth movement, especially when crossing fingers.

ゆっくり ソとラ
Slowly, G and A

先生がたへ
前の曲と同じように。
To the teachers
Always smoothly.

第4プロポジション
No. 4 Proposition

練習曲 44a みぎての ゆびかえし 3-① 1-③の復習
ミ と ファ でかえし

44a Review of crossing fingers 3-① 1-③ of the right hand
　　Crossing the fingers on E and F

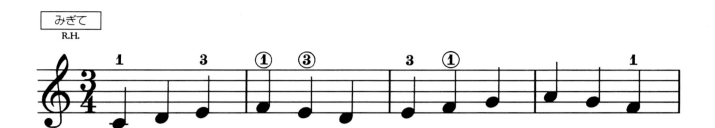

第4プロポジション
No. 4 Proposition

練習曲 44b ひだりての ゆびかえし 3-① 1-③の復習
ラ と ソ でかえし

44b Review of crossing fingers 3-① 1-③ of the left hand
　　Crossing the fingers on A and G

第4プロポジション
No. 4 Proposition

練習曲 44c りょうての ゆびかえし 3-① 1-③の復習
いっしょに かえし
44c Review of crossing fingers 3-① 1-③ of both hands
Crossing the fingers of both hands

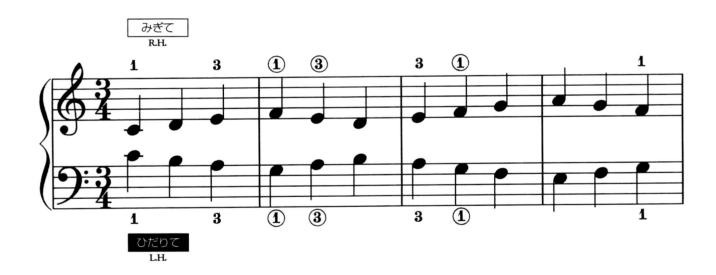

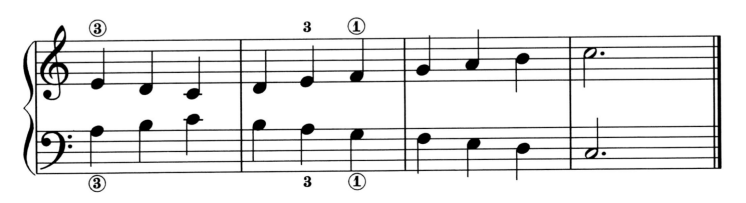

先生がたへ
第3小節、第6小節の弱拍での指かえしは、難しいものです。はじめはそこで力んだりすることもあります。
指かえし運動そのものになれさせ、ゆったりした3拍子の音楽の流れで弾けるよう、導いてあげてください。
To the teacher
Guide the pupil to get used to the movement of crossing fingers, especially on the weak beat at bar 3 and 6 which may be hard for children. Let the music flow in this slow 3/4 piece.

30 第4プロポジション
No. 4 Proposition

練習曲 45 ゆびかえしで やまとなみを
おおきいやま よせるなみ
45 Making a mountain and a wave by crossing fingers
　　A big mountain and surging waves

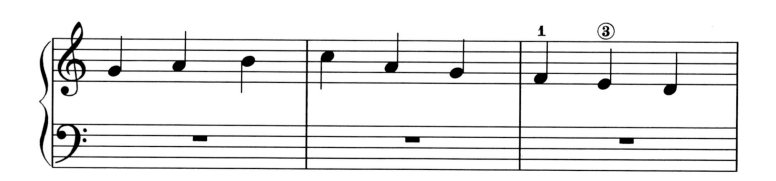

先生がたへ
リピート記号の約束を教えてください。
To the teacher
Teach the pupils about the repeat sign.

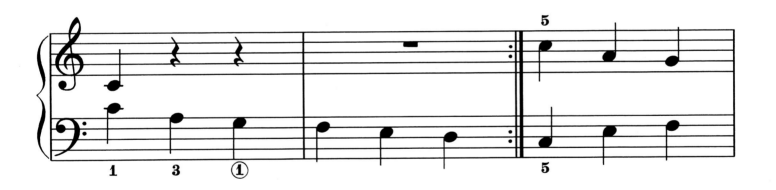

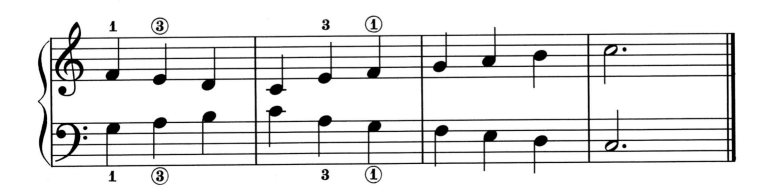

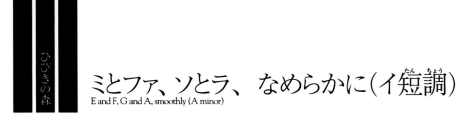

ミとファ、ソとラ、なめらかに（イ短調）
E and F, G and A, smoothly (A minor)

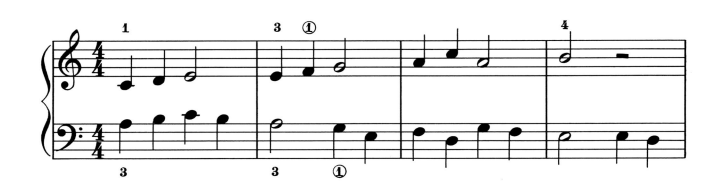

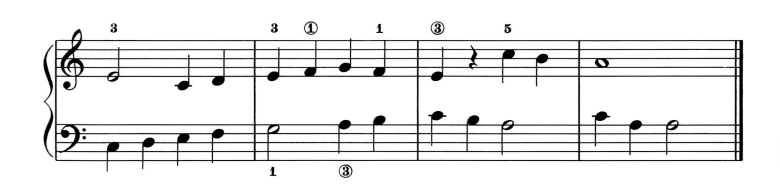

先生がたへ
生徒さんにフレージングを感じとらせ、レガート奏で曲の表情を。
To the teacher
Let your pupil feel the phrase structure and play smoothly to express it.

ミとファ、ソとラ、なめらかに（ハ長調）
E and F, G and A, smoothly (C major)

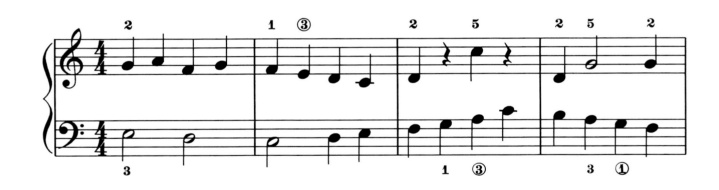

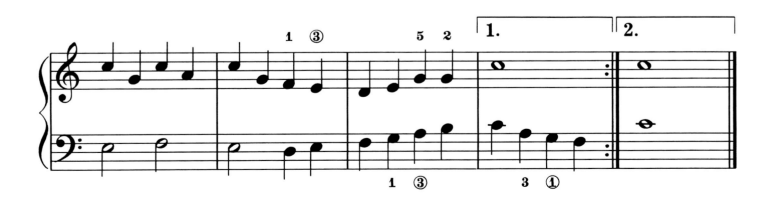

先生がたへ
Andantinoの感じで。3小節目から4小節目の音楽作りが大事です。
To the teacher
Play the piece in Andantino, and express well in bar 3 and 4.

練習曲 46 ゆびかえしの やまのぼり
やっと ついた！

46 Climbing the mountain by crossing fingers
Finally we made it!

はじめは3しょうせつずつレガートに、しずかに。
3だんめからは、**みぎて**と**ひだりて**がなかよく。

At the beginning of the piece, play 3 bars at a time legato and calmly.
From the third line, play with both hands together.

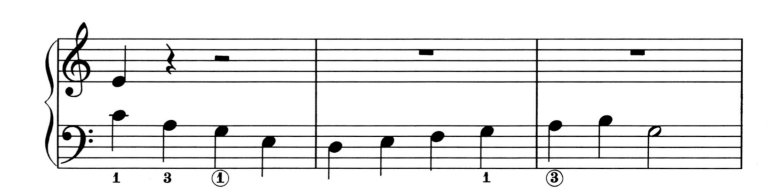

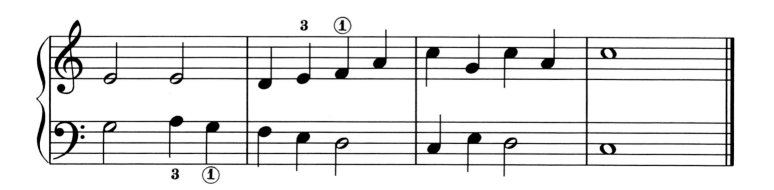

先生がたへ
※印の2-2の指づかいは、あらかじめ、2の指がつづくことを教えておきます。
To the teacher
Draw the pupils' attention to the 2-2 fingering at ※ in advance.

第4プロポジション
No. 4 Proposition

練習曲 47 ゆびかえしの　サーフィン
すてきに のれた！
47 Let's surf by crossing fingers
　Enjoy the wave with spirit!

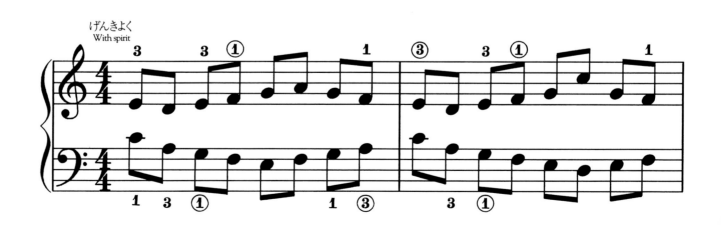

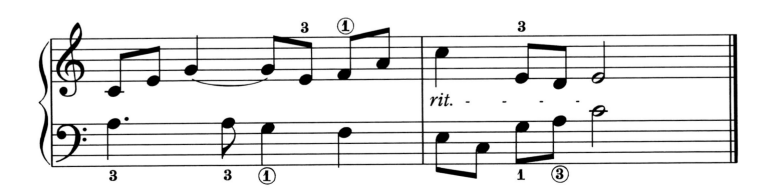

第4プロポジション
No. 4 Proposition

練習曲 48 みぎての ゆびかえし 3-① と 1-③ / 1-④ をつかって

そらたかく

48 Crossing fingers 3-①, 1-③ / 1-④ of the right hand
The sky is so high!

3-①、1-④ の**ゆびかえし**ができると、
どんなとおくの けんばんまでも、
いってかえってくることができますね。

This technique gives you the ability to play a wider range of notes continuously.

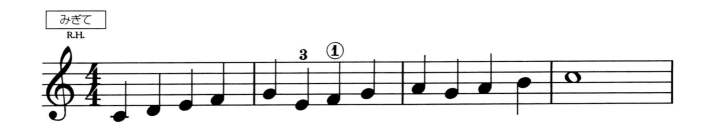

第4プロポジション
No. 4 Proposition

練習曲 49 ひだりての ゆびかえし 3-① と 1-③ / 1-④ をつかって をつかって

うみふかく

49 Crossing fingers 3-①, 1-③ / 1-④ of the left hand
The sea is so deep

ゆびかえしのときも、
けんばんにかける **てのおもさ**が、かわらないように。
3-①、1-④、1-③のとき、
おなじおもさを、1と3と4のゆびが、かんじていますか。

The hand's weight should be supported equally by each finger.
Do you feel the same weight on fingers 1, 3 and 4 when crossing the fingers,
3-①, 1-④, and 1-③?

先生がたへ
肘が下がりすぎていると、手首を無理にまわすことがあります。
椅子の高さや、すわり方に注目し、体全体の安定に気をつけてください。
To the teacher
If the elbow is too low, the wrist may make unnecessary movement.
Ensure that the pupil plays with the correct posture sitting on the stool at the proper height.

練習曲 50　みぎてのゆびかえし 4-①、1-④の変奏
かぜも 7色　(右手)

50 Variations on crossing fingers 4-① 1-④ of the right hand
The wind and seven colors (right hand)

練習曲42で 3-① の**ゆびかえし**をれんしゅうしたように、
みぎての 4-① の**ゆびかえし**も、れんしゅうしてみましょう。
きをつけることは**練習曲42**とおなじです。

Let's practice 4-① with the right hand, as we did 3-① in exercise 42.

練習曲 51 ひだりてのゆびかえし 4-① 1-④の変奏
かぜも 7色 (左手)

51 Variations on crossing the finger 4-① 1-④ of the left hand
The wind and seven colors (left hand)

**練習曲43で 3-① のゆびかえしをれんしゅうしたように、
ひだりての 4-① のゆびかえしも、れんしゅうしてみましょう。
きをつけることは練習曲43とおなじです。**

Let's practice 4-① with the left hand, as we did 3-① in exercise 43.

第4プロポジション
No. 4 Proposition

練習曲 52a みぎてで ファ♯ (シャープ)
シャープさん こんにちは (右手)

52a F♯ with the right hand
Hello, ♯! (right hand)

このきょくの**ファ**は、**2 ことも**♯ (シャープ)がついています。
Note that there are two F♯.

したのがくふのように、<u>五</u>せんのはじめのファのところに♯ (シャープ)をつければ、
↓印↑印**2 こともファ**♯ (シャープ)でひくことになり、
うえのがくふと、おなじおんがくになります。

When a ♯ is at the beginning of the staves as shown below, all Fs are played as F♯.
Can you see that the music above and below are actually the same?

先生がたへ
♯をつけて弾く音に丸をつけさせましょう。

To the teacher
Have your pupil draw a circle around the note played with ♯.

第4プロポジション
No. 4 Proposition

練習曲 52b　ひだりてで ファ♯（シャープ）
シャープさん こんにちは（左手）

52b F♯ with the left hand
Hello, ♯! (left hand)

このきょくでも、2 このファに♯（シャープ）がついていますね。
Can you see that there are also two F♯s here?

このようにかいてもおなじです。
This music can also be written as shown below.

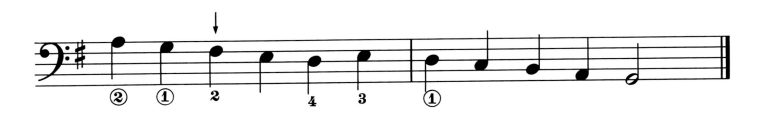

先生がたへ
♯をつけて弾く音に丸をつけさせましょう。
To the teacher
Have your pupil draw a circle around the note played with ♯.

第4プロポジション
No. 4 Proposition

練習曲 52c　ファ♯(シャープ)と 1-③ 3-① のれんしゅう
ちいさな うずまき
52c F♯ and 1-③ 3-① practice
Little swirl

レガートでひきましょう。
みぎてとひだりてでは、レガートのながさがちがいますね。
ゆびかえしのとき、レガートがみだれないように。

Play legato.
Especially when crossing the fingers.
Can you see the different length of the legato for each hand?

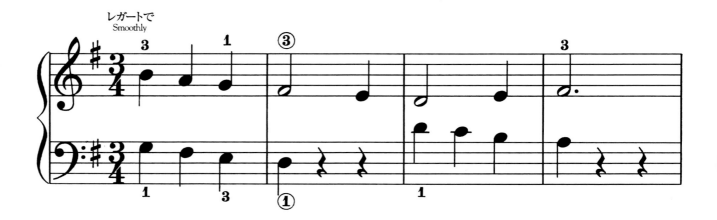

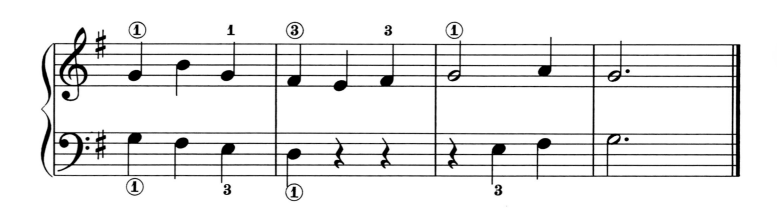

第4プロポジション
No. 4 Proposition

練習曲 52d　ファ♯（シャープ）と 4-① 1-④ のうんどうのれんしゅう
みんなで いこう！
52d F♯ and 4-① 1-④ practice
Come on, everyone!

4-①のゆびかえしを、すばやくできるように、
りょうてとも、うごきのはやいせんりつでれんしゅうしておきましょう。
Now, practice crossing fingers on a fast melody with both hands,
so that you can cross fingers 4-① swiftly.

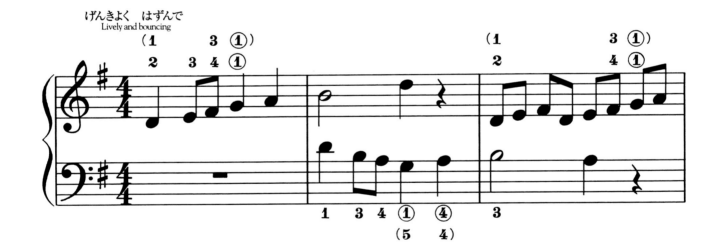

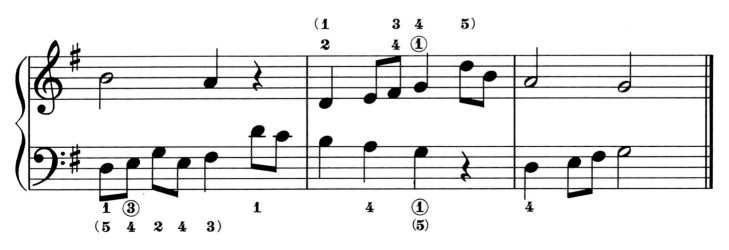

先生がたへ
この指づかいは、指かえしの運動性を高めるためのものです。生徒の様子を見て、難しそうでしたら、**練習曲52e**に進んでください。
また、弾きやすい指づかい（カッコ数字）で弾いてもよいのです。
To the teacher
This fingering aims at enhancing better finger-crossing skill. If your pupils find it difficult,
let them try Exercise 52e, or choose the easier fingering marked with (　).

練習曲 52e　りょうてで ファ♯（シャープ）
ゆうやけ おやすみ

52e F♯ with both hands
Good night, sunset

5 しょうせつめからの　みぎてのせんりつは、
ひだりての　どこにありますか？

Can you find the right hand melody beginning from bar 5 appearing on the left hand?

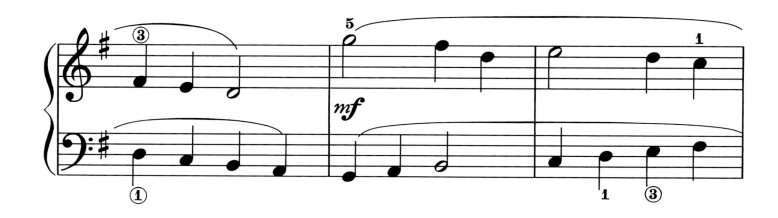

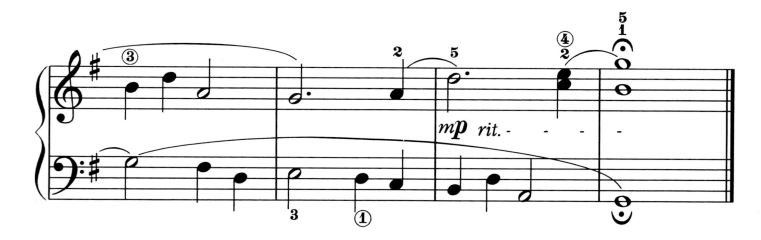

先生がたへ
mf , *mp* は説明をして、その気持ちを感じさせてください。
To the teacher
Explain *mf* , *mp* and let your pupils feel their moods.

発展編
Developing skills

練習曲52eのように、

なめらかにひくやくそくの **スラー**とか、

だんだんつよく(おおきく)したり、

だんだんよわく(ちいさく)したりする、

やくそくのきごうも、でてきます。

おなじおとでも、ひきかたによって、

いろいろな、かんじがだせるのですね。

Now we have more musical terms; slur to play smoothly, crescendo (gradually louder), diminuendo (gradually softer).
You can create different mood with these signs.

先生がたへ
記号は、楽典としてではなくて、約束のしるしとして、おぼえさせてください。気持ちが大事です。
To the teacher
Have your pupils learn the musical terms as means for expression, rather than just the theory. It is important to feel and express.

50 第4プロポジション
No. 4 Proposition

練習曲 53 なめらかな ハ長調のうた
なみの いきき

53 A gentle song in C major
　Waves are going and coming

4-①、1-④ の **ゆびかえし**も
3-①、1-③ の **ゆびかえし**とおなじように、なめらかに。
3 しょうせつめの、ひだりては、
はじめのみぎてのせんりつをおもいうかべて、ひいてください。
3 だんめの 1 しょうせつめのひだりてにも、
おなじようなせんりつがでてくるでしょう？

Cross the fingers smoothly with 4-① and 1-④, just as you did with 3-① and 1-③.
Remember the melody appeared at bar 1 (right hand) when you play bar 3 (left hand).
Can you see a similar melody appearing again at the first bar on the 3rd line(left hand) ?

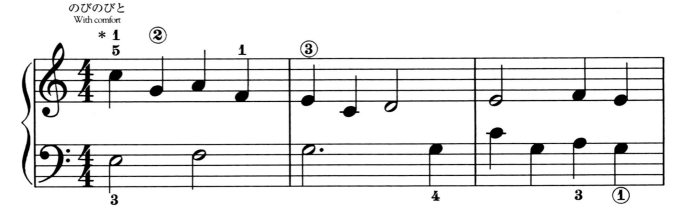

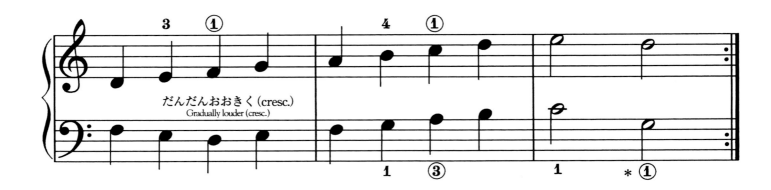

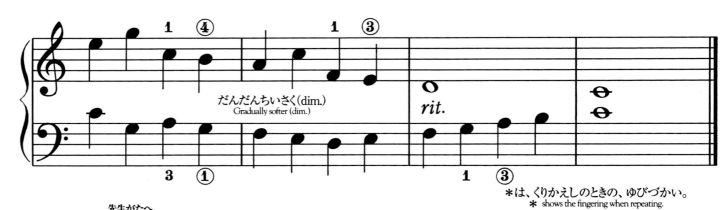

＊は、くりかえしのときの、ゆびづかい。
＊ shows the fingering when repeating.

先生がたへ
機械的な音階練習よりも、肘、下腕、手首、関節の動きに留意しながら、ゆっくりと指かえしの運動イメージを定着させることの方が大切です。
そうして、**練習曲52**でおぼえた*mf*、*mp*の感じを、この曲に取り入れてください。
cresc.、***dim.*** を、もう一度確かめてください。

To the teacher
It is important that your pupil plays this piece slowly to master the movement of finger crossing with attention to the correct posture,
proper movement of the elbows, lower arms, wrists and finger joints.
Let them try to express ***mf***, ***mp***, ***cresc.*** and ***dim.*** with this piece. Confirm the meaning of ***cresc.*** and ***dim.*** once again.

第4プロポジション
No. 4 Proposition

練習曲 54　ト長調で1-②-①のれんしゅう
やさしい つむじかぜ
54 Practicing 1-②-① in G major
　　Gentle whirlwind

3 しょうせつめから、したのだんの 1 しょうせつめにすすむとき、
しぜんに**おとが　おおきくなる**でしょう？
さいごの 2 しょうせつでは、**しぜんにちいさくなりますね。**
となりの音からすぐもどるとき 1 -②-① の**ゆびかえし**もつかいます。
You played gradually louder from bar 3 to the first bar of the lower line,
and the last two bars gradually softer, didn't you?
Crossing finger, 1-②-① is used when you move immediately between the notes next to each other.

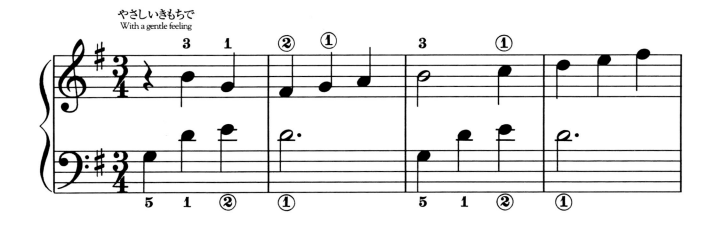

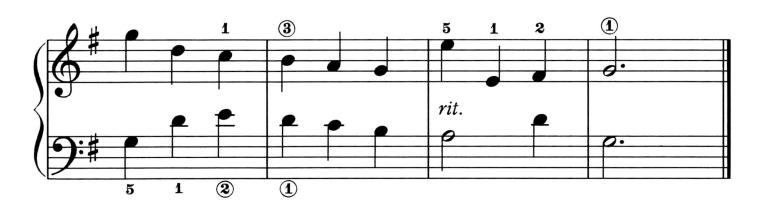

先生がたへ
生徒へのコメントに関連して、*cresc.*，*dim.* の意味を言葉で確かめてください。　また、*mf*，*mp* の感じをとり入れてください。
To the teacher
Discuss the meaning of *cresc.* and *dim.* when you give comment to your pupils, also let them try to express *mf* and *mp* in their playing.

練習曲 55 ながいレガート
すいへいせん

55 Long legato
Horizone

ながい**スラー**ですね。
そこは、ぜんぶ、**レガート**で（なめらかに）ひいてください。
みぎての 1-5、ひだりての 5-1 のオクターヴもレガートに。
きょくのかんじをつかんで、
きょうじゃく（*mf*, *mp*, *p* や ＜ , ＞）を かんがえてください。

You will find long slurs in this piece. Play them all legato(smoothly),
and the octaves of the right-hand 1-5 and left-hand 5-1 also.
Feel the mood of the music, and think about suitable dynamics (*mf*, *mp*, *p*, ＜ , ＞).

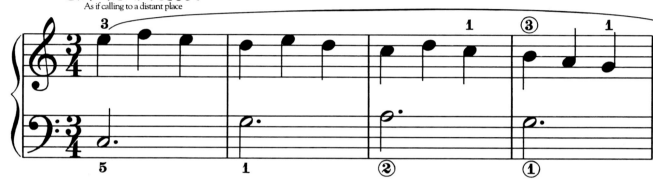

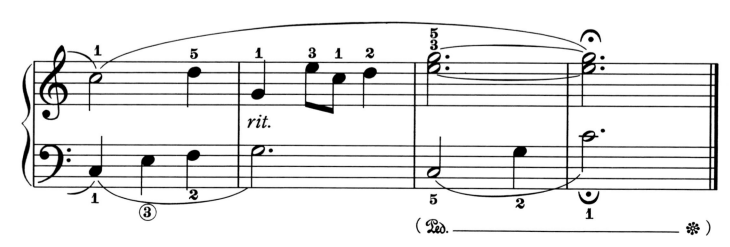

先生がたへ
最後の ℘. は、生徒の余裕があれば（補助ペダルを使っても）、試みてください。

To the teacher
Use the pedal at the end of the piece depending on your pupil's ability. (Supplementary pedal may be used.)

第4プロポジション
No. 4 Proposition

練習曲 56 ゆびをじゆうにうつす
かぜの ものがたり
56 Shifting the fingers
　　The story of the wind

1のゆびが　てのばしょを　きめてくれます。

そのかんじを　あじわいながらひくと

おちついて　えんそうできます。

Finger 1 will tell you the position of your hand.
You can be relaxed if you feel how it is easy to shift the position.

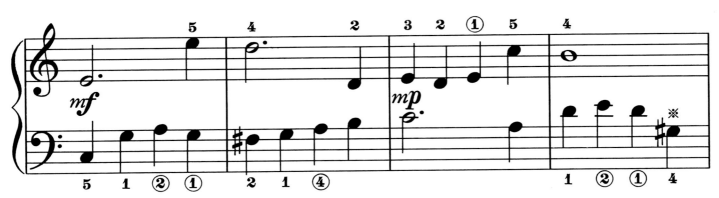

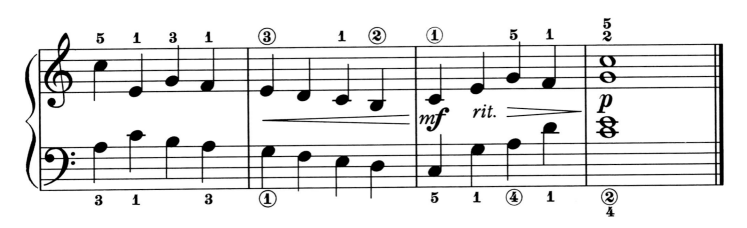

先生がたへ
※印の音は、ソの♯とだけおぼえさせてください。
　mf, *mp*, *p*, ＜ , ＞ , *rit.* の意味と感じを確かめてください。
To the teacher
※Have your pupils learn it simply as the G♯ note. Go over the meaning of the dynamics and *rit.*

練習曲 57 主題の旋律
よろこびの うた

57 Melody of the theme
Joyful song

ながいおんがくですね。
きもちも、おおきくして、ひきはじめてください。
f のところで、はじめのおんがくが、もどってきます。
さいごの 4 しょうせつは、おしまいのおんがくです。
f, *mf*, *mp* のきもちを、たいせつに。

This is a rather long piece, isn't it?
Try to have broad mind to start playing.
The first melody returns at *f* mark and the last four bars make the ending music.
Play with careful attention to the feeling at *f*, *mf*, and *mp* marks.

せんせいによんでいただきましょう。

テヌート（−）のついたおとは、くっきりと、たっぷりと。

＜　　　（クレッシェンド）は、だんだん大きく。

＞　　　（ディミニュエンド）は、だんだん小さく。

Your teacher will explain this to you.
Tenuto : Hold the note clearly and broadly
Crescendo: Gradually louder
Diminuendo: Gradually softer

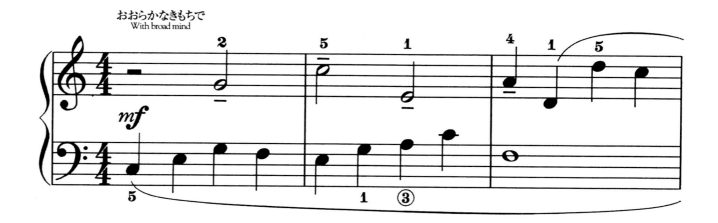

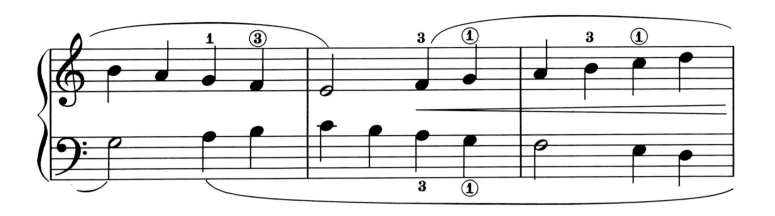
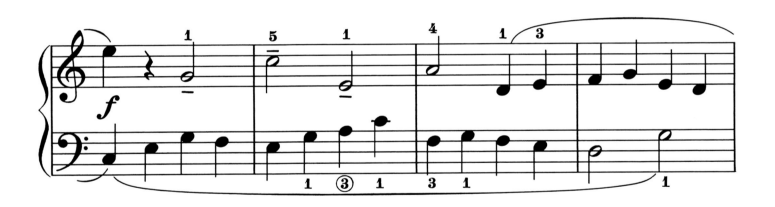
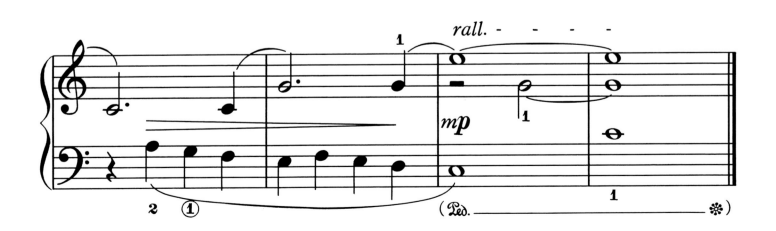

練習曲 58 なめらかなト長調のうた
帆と かぜの うた

58 A flowing song in G major
　The sail and the wind

みぎてに 1 こ、ひだりてに 2 このファがでてきます。
はじめにファの♯がついていますから、3 こともファ♯（ファ・シャープ）ですね。
Note that all Fs are F♯.

先生がたへ
🎵.(ペダル)は、指がその音を弾いたすぐあとに踏みます。
どの音でもいいですから、スタッカートで弾いて、ペダルでその音をのばすことができるかどうか、練習させてください。
To the teacher
Have your pupil practice the pedaling which comes immediately after touching the key.
Try playing staccato and sustain by pedaling.

応用編
Applications

これからひくきょくは、

れんしゅうきょくですが、

きょくのかんじが、

はじめにかいてあります。

ひとつひとつのきょくに、

きょくのなまえをつけてください。

Now you will play some exercise pieces.
The mood of the piece is indicated in the beginning of each piece.
Let's name the title of the pieces.

第4プロポジション
No. 4 Proposition

練習曲 60 イ短調で 右手の重音のリズム奏
[   ]
60 Rhythmic double notes in A minor, right hand
 [   ]

はじめに 3 つあるひだりてのレガートに　きもちをあわせましょう。

そのひだりてが、おんがくをすすめるやくめをしています。

みぎては、それをたすけるきもちで、かるく。

このきょくも、せんせいとのがっそうで、**きょうじゃく**をくふうしてみましょう。

さいごのしょうせつには **rit.** と 𝄐 もあったほうがいいかもしれませんね。

[　　　]のきもちをかんがえてください。

Note the three slurs in the left hand and that the right hand should be played along with them.
Also, think about the dynamics when playing with your teacher.
You may like to use **rit.** and 𝄐 at the end.
Think about and write down a title and the mood of the piece.

先生がたへ
この曲は、右の名前でよびますが、生徒さんの発想で[　　　]の中に曲名をつけてもらってください。
To the teachers
This piece is called "The sunset," but the pupil can select his or her own title.

ゆうひ の うた
The sunset

第4プロポジション
No. 4 Proposition

練習曲 61 左手で 重音を使って合奏
[　　　　　　　　　　]

61 Ensemble using double notes, left hand
[　　　　　　　　　　]

ひだりてとみぎてが、ワルツをひきます。

1 しょうせつごとに、まるい**わ**をえがくきもちで。

4 しょうせつめと、7、8 しょうせつめのひだりても、そのリズムにのせて。

This is a waltz.
Feel the rhythm of the waltz especially at bars 4, 7 and 8.

先生がたへ
ワルツが、ゆるやかに弧を描いて踊る「踊りの音楽」であることを、話してあげてください。
写真や、画を見せてあげたり、先生が踊って見せてくだされば、すばらしい。
また、この曲が長調とも、普通の短調ともちがう感じがすることも、少し話してあげてください。
この曲は、右の名前でよびますが、生徒さんの発想で[　　]の中に曲名をつけてもらってください。

To the teacher
Explain waltzes to your pupil by showing pictures or even dancing a bit. Also explain that this piece sounds different from a usual major or minor key. This piece is called "Circle of the Waltz," but the pupil can select his or her own title.

ワルツの輪
Circle of the Waltz

No. 4 Proposition

練習曲 62 ト長調で 右手の重音の旋律奏
[   ]

62 Melodic double notes in G major, right hand
[   ]

みぎては 4 ぶんおんぷが、とびとびにでてきますが、せんりつは、つづいています。
Note that the melody continues even though there are many rests.

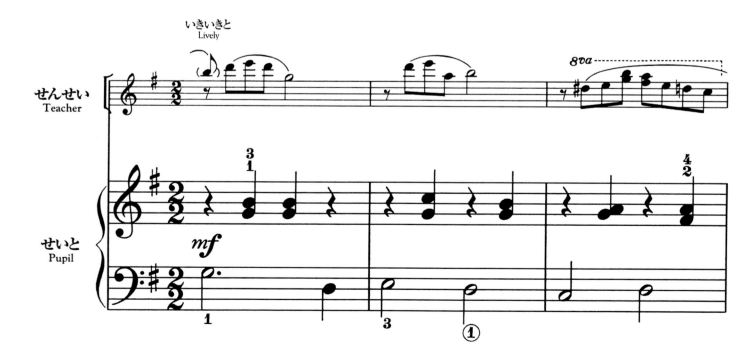

先生がたへ
この曲は、右の名前でよびますが、生徒さんの発想で [　　] の中に曲名をつけてもらってください。
To the teacher
This piece is called "Dance of the ring," but the pupil can select his or her own title.

リングの舞い
Dance of the ring

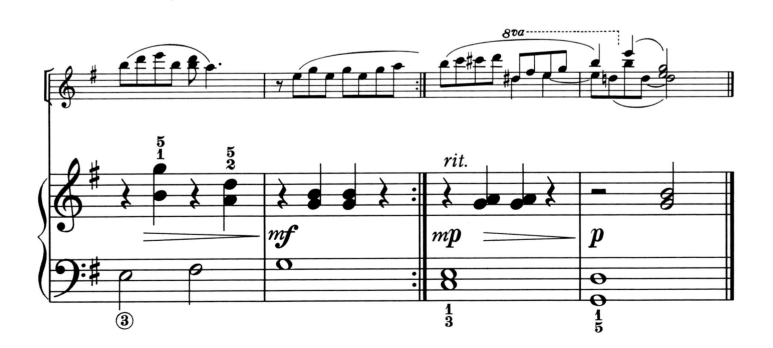

第4プロポジション
No. 4 Proposition

練習曲63 ホ短調で 右手の重音の旋律奏
[　　　　　　　　　]

63 Melodic double notes in E minor, right hand
[　　　　　　　　　]

みぎては、**4ぶんおんぷ**がとびとびにでてきますが、

せんりつはつづいています。

その**せんりつ**と、**ひだりて**のレガートのせんりつとを、

ひびかせあうきもちで。

Note that the melody continues even though there are many rests.
Let's make a good ensemble with the melody and the legato line of the left hand.

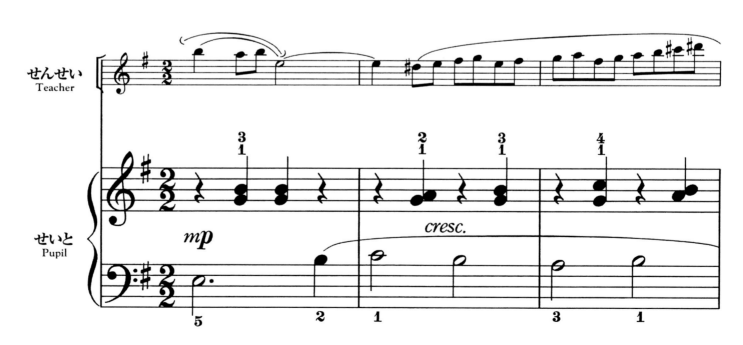

先生がたへ
先生の旋律を合わせる前に、上に書いた気持ちで生徒さんのパートを練習させてください。
この曲は、右の名前でよびますが、生徒さんの発想で[　　]の中に曲名をつけてもらってください。
To the teacher
Have your pupil practice playing with the feeling of the title I have made.
This piece is called "Elegy on crimson," but the pupil can select his or her own title.

茜色のエレジー
Elegy on crimson

復習 おんぷの なかまたち
Review　　　　Friends of notes

$\frac{2}{2}$ は **2 ぶんおんぷのリズム** で、**2 びょうしのおんがく** というしるしでしたね。

おなじように、

$\frac{2}{4}$ は **4 ぶんおんぷのリズム** で、**2 びょうし** ということをあらわしています。

Do you remember that $\frac{2}{2}$ means the piece is in two part time,
having two half notes in a bar as on pages 20, 22 and 38.
Also, $\frac{2}{4}$ means the piece is in two part time, having two quarter notes in a bar.

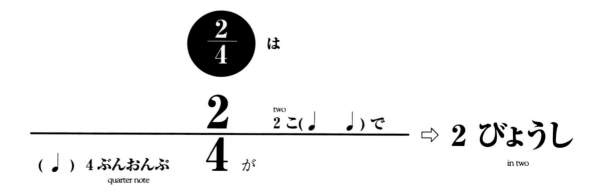

8 ぶんおんぷと 8 ぶんきゅうふ
Eighth notes and rests

2/4 のおんがくでは、

1 しょうせつのなかに、

8 ぶんおんぷや、**8 ぶんきゅうふ**が **4 こ**はいっています。

8 ぶんおんぷ 2 こは、**4 ぶんおんぷ 1 こ**と、**おなじながさ**ですから、

2/4 のおんがくでは、

8 ぶんおんぷや、**8 ぶんきゅうふ**が、

2 こで **1 ぱく**ということになり、

1 しょうせつが **2 はくですすむ**ことになります。

A music in 2/4 has four eighth notes (or rests) in a bar.
The value of two eighth notes equals one quarter note.
Therefore, two eighth notes (rests) make one beat in 2/4 music, and there are two beats in a bar.

8 ぶんおんぷと 8 ぶんきゅうふの ながさのかんけい
Relationship between eighth notes and rests

♪と♪

♩と♪　　　とを、たした**ながさ**は、𝄽や♩と、**おなじながさ**で、**1 ぱく**です。

♪と♩

2/4 になる おんぷのくみあわせを かいてみましょう。

The value of two eighth notes equals one quarter note.
Let's write a 2/4 rhythm using quarter and eighth notes (rests).

たとえば
for example

第4プロポジション
No. 4 Proposition

練習曲 66 ト長調の対位法
[   ]

66 Counterpoint in G major
[   ]

おなじようなせんりつを、りょうてでひきます。

レガートのばしょがちがいますね。

はじめにかたてずつひいて、

みぎてとひだりて、それぞれのかんじをおぼえましょう。

Similar melodies appear for both hands, with legato appearing in a different place. Practice separately and express each line.

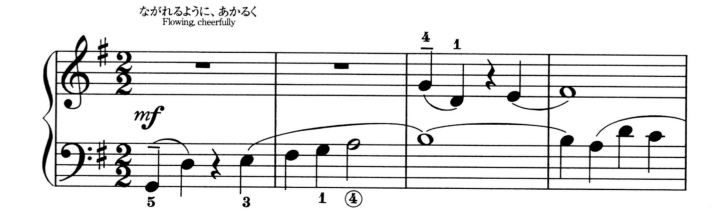

ながれるように、あかるく
Flowing, cheerfully

先生がたへ
[–] テヌートの弾き方を説明してあげてください。腕の重みをかけ、2拍目で抜くように。
この曲は、右の名前でよびますが、生徒さんの発想で [   ] の中に曲名をつけてもらってください。

To the teacher
Explain the meaning of tenuto, which is played with the arm's weight and a release at the second beat.
This piece is called "Joy comes and goes," but the pupil can select his or her own title.

いきかう よろこび
Joy comes and goes

第4プロポジション
No. 4 Proposition

練習曲 67 ホ短調で両手のうた
[　　　　　　　　　　　　]

67 A song in E minor for both hands
[　　　　　　　　　]

かなしみの うみ、なぐさめの かぜ
Sea of sorrow, wind of comfort

おなじようなせんりつを、りょうてでひきます。

レガートのばしょが、ちがいますね。

はじめに、かたてずつひいて、

みぎてとひだりて、それぞれのかんじをおぼえましょう。

Similar melodies appear for both hands, with legato appearing in a different place.
Practice separately and express each line.

せんりつを、いきながく、うたうように（カンタービレ）
Like singing, cantabile

先生がたへ
生徒に曲想（音楽の感じ）をきいてみてください。そのとき、曲想標示も参考にしてください。
この曲は、右の名前でよびますが、生徒さんの発想で[　　]の中に曲名をつけてもらってください。
To the teacher
Ask your pupil about the mood of the music, referring to the expression sign.
This piece is called "Sea of sorrow, wind of comfort," but the pupil can select his or her own title.

かなしみの うみ、なぐさめの かぜ
Sea of sorrow, wind of comfort

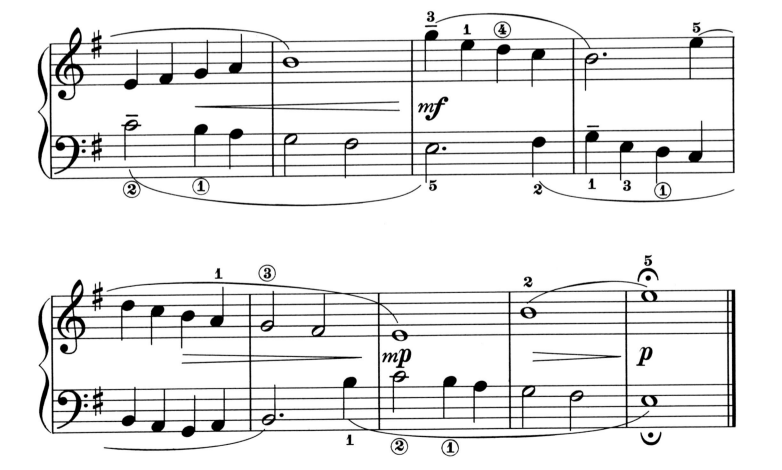

おんがくのことばとやくそく
Musical terms and rules

楽典
Theory

1.音名
Note names

ド	レ	ミ	ファ	ソ	ラ	シ	ド
C	D	E	F	G	A	B	C

日本名で ハ 二 ホ ヘ ト イ ロ ハ

2.調性記号
Key signature

五線のはじめの**ファ**のところに ♯（シャープ）をつけると

その曲の**ファ**は、**ファ♯** でひく やくそくになります。
When a ♯ sign is at the beginning of the staves, all Fs are played as F♯.

白鍵ばかりでひく音楽は、音の仲間が、
There are two scales which use only white keys:

「**ド** - **レ** - **ミ** - **ファ** - **ソ** - **ラ** - **シ** - **ド**」と、
C D E F G A B C

「**ラ** - **シ** - **ド** - **レ** - **ミ** - **ファ** - **ソ** - **ラ**」
A B C D E F G A

の2組ありました。

ファが**ファ♯（シャープ）**になる音楽は、音の仲間が、
There are also two scales which use only white keys and F♯:

「**ソ** - **ラ** - **シ** - **ド** - **レ** - **ミ** - **ファ♯** - **ソ**」と
G A B C D E C G

「**ミ** - **ファ♯** - **ソ** - **ラ** - **シ** - **ド** - **レ** - **ミ**」
E F♯ G A B C D E

の2組あります。

白鍵ばかりで、**ド**から**ド**までの音楽は、**ハ長調**（ハはド）です。**(練習曲59)**
The scale using only the white keys, beginning and ending on C is called C major (Exercise 59).

白鍵ばかりで、**ラ**から**ラ**までの音楽は、**イ短調**（イはラ）です。**(練習曲60、61)**
The scale using only the white keys, beginning and ending on A is called A minor (Exercise 60 and 61).

ファが**ファ♯**（シャープ）になる、**ソ**から**ソ**までの音楽は、**ト長調**（トはソ）です。**(練習曲62、64、66)**
The scale using the white keys and F♯, beginning and ending on G is called G major (Exercises 62, 64 and 66).

ファが**ファ♯**（シャープ）になる、**ミ**から**ミ**までの音楽は、**ホ短調**（ホはミ）です。**(練習曲63、65、67)**
The scale using the white keys and F♯, beginning and ending on E is called E minor (Exercise 63, 65 and 67).